KU-012-579

# Animal Neighbours

# Blackbird

## Stephen Savage

HODDER
Wayland

An imprint of Hodder Children's Books

# Animal Neighbours

## Titles in this series:

## Badger • Bat • Blackbird • Deer • Duck • Fox Hare • Hedgehog • Mole • Mouse • Otter • Owl Rat • Snake • Swallow • Toad

For more information on this series and other Hodder Wayland titles,
go to www.hodderwayland.co.uk

Conceived and produced for Hodder Wayland by

### Nutshell
MEDIA

Intergen House, 65–67 Western Road, Hove BN3 2JQ, UK
www.nutshellmedialtd.co.uk

Commissioning Editor: Vicky Brooker
Design: Mayer Media Ltd
Illustrator: Jackie Harland
Picture Research: Glass Onion Pictures

Published in Great Britain in 2005 by Hodder Wayland, an imprint of Hodder Children's Books.

© Copyright 2005 Hodder Wayland

All rights reserved. Apart from any use permitted under UK copyright law, this publication may only be reproduced, stored or transmitted, in any form, or by any means with prior permission in writing of the publishers or in the case of reprographic production in accordance with the terms of licences issued by the Copyright Licensing Agency.

British Library Cataloguing in Publication Data
Savage, Stephen, 1965-
Blackbird. – (Animal neighbours)
1. European blackbird – Juvenile literature
I. Title
589.9'42

ISBN 0 7502 4662 6

Cover: A blackbird swallowing a hawthorn berry.
Title page: A male blackbird singing to attract a female.

### Picture acknowledgements
FLPA 6 (Richard Brooks), 8 (Mike Jones), 9 (Roger Wilmshurst), 10 (E & D Hosking), 11 (David Hosking), 26 (Silvestris), 28 top (Mike Jones), 28 right (David Hosking);
OSF 23 (Carlos Sanchez Alonso), 27 (Ian West), 28 left (Carlos Sanchez Alonso);
naturepl.com 7 (Jose B. Ruiz), 12 (Kevin Keatley), 13 (Ross Hoddinott), 21 (Steve Knell), 25 (Martin H. Smith), 28 bottom (Ross Hoddinott);
NHPA 17 (Manfred Danegger), 22 (Ernie Janes), 24 (Michael Leach);
rspb-images.com Cover (Richard Brooks), Title page (Laurie Campbell), 14 (Richard Brooks), 15 (Chris Gomersall), 16 (Laurie Campbell), 19 (Richard Brooks), 20 (Ray Kennedy).

Printed and bound in China.

Hodder Children's Books
A division of Hodder Headline Limited
338 Euston Road, London NW1 3BH

# Contents

# Meet the Blackbird

The blackbird is a member of the thrush family, a group of songbirds that produce beautiful sounds. They live in a variety of habitats including woodland, open countryside, gardens, parks and churchyards.

This book looks at the European blackbird, one of the most familiar garden birds.

▲ The red shading on this map shows where the European blackbird lives in the world today.

## BLACKBIRD FACTS

The blackbird's scientific name is *Turdus merula*, which comes from the Latin words *turdus* meaning 'thrush' and *merula* meaning 'blackbird'.

The blackbird's common name comes from the jet-black colour of the male. The female blackbird is brown.

Male blackbirds are called cocks and females are called hens. The young are called chicks.

Males and females are the same size, about 24–25 cm long. They have a wingspan of 34–38 cm and weigh 80–125 g.

### Tail

The tail helps the blackbird change direction in the air. It may also be raised upright when singing, or when a male confronts another male.

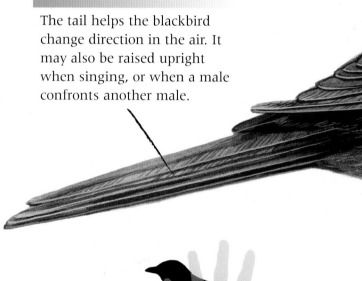

▲ This shows the size of the blackbird compared to an adult human hand.

## Ears

The blackbird's ears do not have an external flap. Instead, a small hole leads to an inner ear, which is used to hear other blackbird calls and sounds of danger.

## Eyes

Blackbirds have eyes on the sides of their heads, which helps them spot prey and predators all around them. Male blackbirds have an orange ring around their eyes to attract females.

## Beak

The strong beak is used for probing soil and picking up food. It is normally brown, but in the breeding season male blackbirds have orange beaks.

▼ A male blackbird.

## Nostrils

The nostrils are at the base of the beak so the blackbird can breathe while eating and drinking.

## Body

Blackbirds have the plump body shape of a bird that feeds on the ground, compared to the streamlined shape of swallows and other birds that feed mid-air.

## Feathers

The male blackbird has jet-black feathers, whereas the female is brown with speckled chest feathers. Small, contoured feathers on the body keep the blackbird warm, while long, streamlined feathers on the wings help flight.

## Legs and feet

Blackbirds have strong legs with four toes. Three toes point forwards and one points backwards. This arrangement allows the blackbird to perch on branches and stand on the ground.

# The Blackbird Family

There are 160 species in the thrush family, including blackbirds, robins and thrushes. All members of this family have a rounded body, long legs and a slender beak. The males have beautiful songs, which they use to communicate with other birds of the same species.

The nightingale is the best-known singer of the family, with its rich melodies and warbling trills. The male sings during the day to defend his territory and is often heard on warm summer evenings, singing to attract a female.

## IMMIGRANTS

In the late nineteenth century, when Europeans started to settle in Australia and New Zealand, they took blackbirds with them. They released the blackbirds into the wild so that they would hear some familiar sounds as well as the strange sounds of the native birds. Descendents of these blackbirds are still alive in Australia and New Zealand today.

◀ The nightingale spends the summer in parts of Europe before flying south to spend the winter in West Africa.

Birds of the thrush family find most of their food on the ground. The European song thrush was named after its beautiful song, but it is best known for the way it eats snails. It picks them up with its beak and hits them repeatedly against a stone until the shell breaks and it can eat the flesh inside.

While most thrush family members are brown or black, a few have bright markings. Both the European and the American robin have a bright red breast. The colour is used to warn other males away from a robin's territory and to attract females.

▼ The song thrush is one of the few birds that can crack open a snail's shell.

# Birth and Growing Up

It is spring, and a male and female blackbird gather mud, grasses and leaves to build a nest. They choose a site above the ground, out of reach of predators. This may be in a tree, deep within a hedge, or hidden behind ivy growing on a wall.

## EGGS

**Blackbird eggs are pale bluish-green with reddish blotches.**

**A group of eggs is called a clutch. A group of chicks is called a brood.**

**There can be between three and five eggs in a clutch.**

Over the next few days, the female lays one egg in the nest each day. When the last egg has been laid, she sits on the eggs to keep them warm and safe while the chicks grow inside. Each egg's hard, outer layer protects the chick while the yolk inside provides all the food the chick needs until it is ready to hatch.

▼ **This blackbird's nest is hidden in undergrowth beside a garden wall.**

▲ The brood patch on the female's belly helps to keep the eggs warm. This area of the female's body has fewer feathers, so the heat from her warm blood is closer to the eggs.

The female will incubate her eggs in this way for about twelve days, until they are ready to hatch. Meanwhile, the male brings the female food and stands guard nearby. After twelve days, the chicks start to peck their way through the tough eggshell using the special egg tooth on their beaks.

# Early days

▲ These chicks are only two days old so their eyes are still tightly closed.

The newly hatched chicks are born with their eyes closed and only a few downy feathers on their bodies. Too weak to stand at first, they lie quietly in the bottom of the nest. The female continues to incubate them, to keep them warm and hide them from predators. Soon she will leave to find food.

Both the male and the female blackbird collect food for their chicks, taking it in turns to hunt while the other guards the nest. They carry back earthworms, caterpillars and other invertebrates in their beaks.

When the parent birds arrive back at the nest, the hungry chicks sense their presence. They compete with each other for food, standing up in the nest and calling out with their mouths wide open. The inside of each chick's beak is bright orange, so when they open their mouths they flash a signal to their parents to feed them. When a chick has had enough to eat it will settle down and rest.

▼ Chicks get all the drinking water they need from worms, whose bodies are made up mostly of water.

When the chicks are about 7 days old their eyes open for the first time. Over the next week, the chicks grow quickly, developing feathers that are brown with speckled markings.

## SURVIVAL OF THE FITTEST

Sometimes, not all the chicks in a brood survive their first week. The parents always feed the chicks with the loudest call and brightest gape first, to make sure that at least some of the brood will survive. This means that weaker chicks are the last to be fed, and some will die of starvation when food is in short supply.

# Leaving the nest

By the time they are 2 weeks old, the young blackbirds are ready to start leaving the nest. Since they are not yet able to fly, they stay in the branches near the nest or hide in vegetation on the ground.

The young birds flutter about awkwardly at first as they exercise their flight muscles. Their first flights are short and clumsy. This is a dangerous time for the young blackbirds because without the ability to fly, they cannot escape from predators. After two more days, the young birds are able to fly. They are now called fledgelings.

▼ By the time the young birds are 2 weeks old the nest is overcrowded. It is time for them to leave.

Adult blackbirds make special calls in times of danger. The main alarm call is a 'chink-chink' sound that they use to alert other blackbirds to a predator nearby. A blackbird may also use this call to lure a predator away from its chicks. Parent blackbirds use a 'chock-chock' call to warn their chicks to stay still.

The parent blackbirds continue to feed the fledgelings for up to three weeks, while they learn to find food for themselves. If the female is back on the nest ready to lay another clutch of eggs, much of this feeding will be done by the male.

By the time they are 3 weeks old, young blackbirds are able to look after themselves and leave their parents' territory. If there is enough food available, most young blackbirds travel no further than 1–2 kilometres away.

◄ All young blackbirds are brown with speckled feathers. This fledgeling is perched on the handle of a spade.

# Habitat

Several hundred years ago, blackbirds in Europe lived mainly in woodland, which covered most of the land. As much of this woodland was cut down to make way for farmland, towns and cities, blackbirds had to find new homes.

Today blackbirds live in many different habitats. In the countryside, they still prefer woodland edges and natural clearings, where the trees offer nest and roost sites hidden from predators. But hedgerows on farmland are also popular, since they also provide nest sites with open feeding areas nearby.

▼ On woodland edges, blackbirds can feed on the ground and fly to the safety of the trees if a predator approaches.

## PERCHING

Blackbirds are a type of perching bird, which means they can grip branches and other objects. When a blackbird lands on an object its legs bend, which makes its tendons tighten and its toes close around the object. Blackbirds can sleep perched on a branch in this way. The tendons remain locked until the blackbird launches itself from the perch, straightening its legs and relaxing its tendons, which releases the toes' grip.

▲ A male blackbird perches on the edge of a flowerpot with a worm in its beak.

In towns and cities, blackbirds live in parks, churchyards, or other open spaces with trees or bushes nearby. In both towns and the countryside, blackbirds are regular visitors to gardens.

At night, blackbirds roost in trees or bushes. They usually roost on their own, but in winter, some spend the night in communal roosts. By roosting together, blackbirds keep each other warm. They may also pass on information to each other about good places to feed.

# Territory

During their first year, male blackbirds find a territory, which they may keep throughout their lives. They look for an area that has good nest and roost sites, as well as access to food and water.

▼ This male blackbird is singing from a high branch of an apple tree.

Males defend their territory against rival males throughout the breeding season, which may start as early as March and finish in July. They warn other males to stay away by singing from posts around their territory. The singing posts may be branches of trees or the roofs of houses.

▲ **Two male blackbirds fight over an apple. During a cold winter, squabbles can easily break out between neighbouring birds.**

When two males meet on the ground, they try and scare each other away. Both birds stare at one another with their tails erect until one flies away. Male blackbirds rarely get close enough to fight because they will avoid injury whenever possible. They know that if they were to get injured, they would soon die.

## MIGRANTS

Birds that stay in the same place all year round are called residents. Not all blackbirds stay in the same place throughout the year. In the winter, blackbirds from parts of Scandinavia, Germany and Poland travel south to warmer parts of Europe, such as Britain and France. These migrants often roost together with resident blackbirds for warmth and safety. In early spring, the migrants return to their original country to breed.

# Food

Blackbirds are omnivores. They eat a wide variety of food, including earthworms, insects, and fruit. They feed mainly on the ground, using their strong, slender beaks to probe the soil. The blackbird's favourite food is earthworms. Since an earthworm's body is made up of 85 per cent water, they are an important source of drinking water as well as food.

▼ **The blackbird is at the centre of its food chain. (The illustrations are not to scale.)**

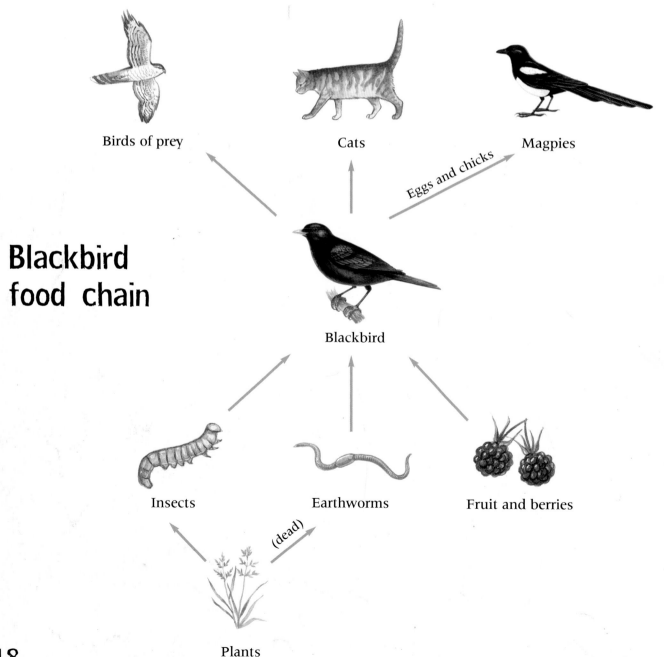

**Blackbird food chain**

Birds of prey

Cats

Magpies

Eggs and chicks

Blackbird

Insects

Earthworms

Fruit and berries

(dead)

Plants

The blackbird's diet varies at different times of the year according to the food available. In the spring and summer, insects and earthworms are a favourite food. Blackbirds also eat tadpoles from the edges of ponds.

In the summer and autumn, ripe fruits such as blackberries, cherries and apples are eaten. In the winter, when insects become scarce and the ground is too hard to find worms, the berries from holly and ivy provide essential food.

▼ A blackbird eats ripe apples straight from the tree. Blackbirds also eat fruit after it has fallen to the ground.

# Foraging

In villages, towns and cities, blackbirds forage for food in gardens, parks and churchyards. In gardens, blackbirds eat bread and fruit from bird tables. Garden ponds and bird baths can also be important sources of water, for drinking or bathing.

Playing fields and lawns are a good source of earthworms and insects, but blackbirds will only forage around the edges of open areas so that they can fly up to a nearby tree, hedge or wall at the first sign of danger. Blackbirds that live in woodlands hunt for earthworms in grassy clearings deep within the woods, or on the edges of a nearby field.

▼ Bird tables give blackbirds a high feeding platform where they will be safer from cats.

▲ This female blackbird has collected a whole beak full of worms which she will carry back to feed her chicks.

## CATCHING WORMS

When a blackbird searches for worms, it makes several short hopping runs, stopping in between to look for any signs of movement. Since its eyes are on the side of its head, the blackbird cocks its head to one side for a better look. When it sees a worm, the bird darts forward, pulls it out of the ground with its beak and swallows it whole.

Garden blackbirds can become quite tame, eating or collecting worms turned up by gardeners as they dig. People who feed garden birds sometimes find that a tame blackbird will learn to tap on their window with its beak when it is hungry.

# Finding a Mate

▼ This male
blackbird is singing
to attract a female.

Blackbirds are ready to breed by the time they are one
year old. At the start of the breeding season, which
can be as early as February, males attract females
using their flute-like song. Blackbirds start to nest
earlier than many other birds, so their song is one of
the earliest bird songs of the year.

The female is first attracted by the quality and length
of a male blackbird's song. Once in sight, she will
notice if the male has glossy feathers, and a bright
orange beak and eye ring. These are all signs that the
male is fit and healthy enough to produce
strong, healthy chicks.

## BIRD SONG

Songbirds produce sounds using their
syrinx, which is a special organ attached to
their windpipe. Air passes through the two
chambers of the syrinx on its way to the lungs,
producing beautiful
sounds. Having two
chambers means that
birds can sing two
different notes at the
same time. Some
songbirds, including
the blackbird, can
mimic sounds such as
car alarms and telephones.

Syrinx

Lungs          Windpipe

Once the female has accepted the male, she chooses a nest site and both the male and the female build the nest. They usually build a new nest, but occasionally a pair will rebuild a damaged nest from the previous year. When the nest is complete, the two blackbirds will mate.

Blackbird pairs usually raise two broods a year, but three or more broods is common. Male blackbirds will often pair up and mate with the same female each year.

▼ **This female blackbird is using her beak to collect and carry materials to make her nest.**

# Threats

Blackbirds can live up to the age of 20 years, but most only live for three or four years. Their most dangerous time is during the breeding season, when predators kill their eggs and young, or the adults cannot find enough food for themselves and their chicks.

In the countryside, the blackbird's main predators are birds of prey, such as sparrowhawks and tawny owls. Sparrowhawks hunt and kill blackbirds in the daytime, on the ground or in the air. Tawny owls attack them at night, when they are asleep.

◀ **This sparrowhawk has caught and killed an adult blackbird almost half its size.**

▲ When hedgerows are cut in the autumn, berries that birds rely on are destroyed.

During cold winters or hot summers, food or water can become scarce in the countryside. A visit to a garden bird table can literally save a blackbird's life. When there is little food available, blackbirds cannot raise as many broods.

Much of the blackbird's habitat has been destroyed by modern farming techniques. Tractors and other farm machinery need bigger fields and thousands of kilometres of hedgerows have been cut down over the last 50 years. Farmers also spray chemical pesticides on their crops, which wipe out the blackbird's insect prey.

## 'SING A SONG OF SIXPENCE'

Between the 15th and 17th centuries, blackbird pie was a delicacy in Europe. It took between 20 and 30 blackbirds to make each pie. The nursery rhyme 'Sing a song of sixpence' is based on a true story in a king's court. The cook baked a pie crust and placed it over some live blackbirds as a joke, to surprise and entertain the king. When the pie was cut, the blackbirds flew out.

# Urban threats

In towns and cities, natural predators such as crows, magpies and domestic cats are the blackbird's biggest threats, especially to young birds. Cats are good climbers and can often reach a blackbird's nest. Crows and magpies are a particular danger to blackbird eggs and chicks, which they steal from the nest.

▼ This carrion crow has just stolen eggs from a blackbird's nest.

Another threat in towns and cities is road traffic, especially to blackbirds flying low. Pesticides used in parks and gardens can also kill the blackbird's insect prey.

# CATS

Domestic cats were first brought into Europe by the Romans in about AD 300, in order to catch mice. They are now a serious threat to blackbirds and many other birds living in towns and cities. There are around 400 million domestic cats worldwide today and 9 million in the UK alone. Cat owners can help to protect wild birds by putting a bell on their cat's collar, so that birds are given lots of warning when the cat is nearby.

In urban habitats, food is less of a problem to blackbirds because of the extra food and water available from gardens. You can help blackbirds by putting out food for them.

The best foods to put out are bread and fruit. These should be positioned in a place sheltered from the weather but away from a fence or wall, where cats can easily leap up. A bird bath in a garden provides essential water for drinking and bathing, when natural sources have either dried up or frozen.

**This agile cat has climbed up a ▶ bird table, but luckily the birds have already flown.**

# Blackbird Life Cycle

**1** Blackbird eggs hatch after an incubation of 14 days. The chicks are born with their eyes closed and few feathers.

**5** The next spring, when they are a year old, the young blackbirds are ready to mate themselves.

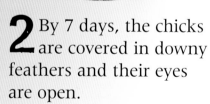

**2** By 7 days, the chicks are covered in downy feathers and their eyes are open.

**4** The parents feed the fledgelings for another three weeks, until they can find food for themselves.

**3** By the time they are 14 days old, the young blackbirds are fully fledged and start to leave the nest.

# Blackbird Clues

Look out for the following clues to help you find a blackbird:

### Nest
The round nest is made from mud and lined with grasses. The nests are easiest to spot in the autumn or winter, when the leaves have fallen from many trees. Never touch a nest when it is being used, but you can pick up a nest that has fallen from a tree since it will not be used again.

### Feeding
A good time to see blackbirds is when they are feeding on fields, lawns and underneath hedgerows. They may also visit garden bird tables and birdbaths.

### Eggshells
Sometimes eggs fall out of the nest or are broken by a predator. Pale green-blue eggshells with red blotches may be found on the ground near a nest.

### Scrapes
When blackbirds look for food in loose soil or leaf litter, they leave shallow holes where the soil has been scraped away. You can often see these scrapes in parks or gardens.

### Footprints
Blackbird footprints can be seen in loose soil or snow. They show the three toes pointing forwards and one toe pointing backwards.

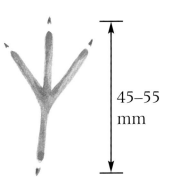

45–55 mm

### Song
Blackbirds sing a flute-like song, which can often be heard in gardens and parks throughout the day. It can even be heard after dark. A blackbird's song is also part of the dawn chorus, when many birds sing at dawn to show their territory is still occupied. When a blackbird feels threatened, it gives a warning call that sounds like 'chink-chink'.

### Feathers
Blackbird feathers can be found at the end of summer, when they moult. Blackbirds moult their feathers at the end of the breeding season, a few at a time until they have all been replaced. The male feathers are black, while the female feathers are a speckled brown.

### Silhouette
The blackbird has a distinctive silhouette when singing in a tree or on a rooftop. The body is rounded while the tail is often held upwards.

# Glossary

**birds of prey**  Birds that eat other animals.

**brood**  A number of chicks produced from one hatching.

**chick**  A young bird.

**clutch**  A number of eggs laid at the same time by one female.

**cock**  A male bird.

**contoured**  Feathers that form the outline of a bird's body shape.

**downy**  Soft and fluffy.

**fledgeling**  The stage in a young bird's life when it has just learnt to fly.

**forage**  To search for food.

**gape**  The opening of a young bird's mouth to show the bright colour inside.

**habitat**  The area where an animal or plant naturally lives.

**hen**  A female bird.

**incubate**  To hatch eggs by sitting on them to keep them warm.

**invertebrates**  Small animals that do not have a backbone. Insects, slugs and spiders are invertebrates.

**leaf litter**  The dead leaves that collect underneath trees or hedgerows.

**migrants**  Animals that make a journey from one region to another in particular seasons.

**moult**  When an animal sheds its fur or feathers to be replaced by new ones.

**omnivores**  Animals that eat both plants and other animals.

**pesticides**  Chemical poisons used by people to kill animals they consider to be pests.

**predator**  An animal that eats other animals.

**prey**  Animals that are killed and eaten by predators.

**resident**  An animal that lives in the same area or country all the time.

**roost**  To gather to rest or sleep.

**silhouette**  The outline of a dark image against a lighter background.

**streamlined**  Shaped to help fly through the air with little effort.

**tendons**  Bands of tough tissue that attach muscles to bone.

**territory**  The area that is defended and controlled by an animal.

**vegetation**  Various different plants that grow together, forming a covering on the ground.

**wingspan**  The distance between the wingtips of a flying animal.

# Finding Out More

## Other books to read

*Animal Classification* by Polly Goodman (Hodder Wayland, 2004)

*Animal Young: Birds* by Rod Theodorou (Heinemann, 1999)

*Classifying Living Things: Classifying Birds* by Andrew Solway (Heinemann, 2003)

*From Egg to Adult: The Life Cycle of Birds* by Mike Unwin (Heinemann, 2003)

*Illustrated Encyclopedia of Animals* by Fran Pickering (Chrysalis, 2003)

*Junior Nature Guides: Birds* (Chrysalis, 2001)

*Life Cycles: Ducks and Other Birds* by Sally Morgan (Chrysalis, 2001)

*Living Nature: Birds* by Angela Royston (Chrysalis, 2002)

*The Wayland Book of Common British Birds* by Nick Williams (Hodder Wayland, 2000)

*What's the Difference?: Birds* by Stephen Savage (Hodder Wayland, 2002)

*Wild Britain: Towns & Cities, Parks & Gardens* by R. & L. Spilsbury (Heinemann, 2003)

*Wild Habitats of the British Isles: Hedgerows; Towns & Cities; Woodlands* by R. & L. Spilsbury (Heinemann, 2005)

## Organisations to contact

**Countryside Foundation for Education**
PO Box 8, Hebden Bridge HX7 5YJ
www.countrysidefoundation.org.uk
An organisation that produces training and teaching materials to help the understanding of the countryside and its problems.

**English Nature**
Northminster House, Peterborough, Cambridgeshire PE1 1UA
www.englishnature.org.uk
A government body that promotes the conservation of English wildlife and the natural environment.

**RSPB**
The Lodge, Sandy, Bedfordshire SG19 2DL
www.rspb.org.uk
A wild birds conservation charity with wildlife reserves and a website that includes an A-Z of UK birds, news, surveys and webcams about issues concerning wild birds.

**Wildlife Watch**
National Office, The Kiln, Waterside, Mather Road, Newark NG24 1WT
www.wildlifetrusts.org
The junior branch of the Wildlife Trusts, a network of local Wildlife Trusts caring for nearly 2,500 nature reserves, from rugged coastline to urban wildlife havens, protecting a huge number of habitats and species.

# Index

Page numbers in **bold** refer to a photograph or illustration.